Old ULVERSTON

by
Delya M. Randall

For those not in the know, the message on this postcard translates as 'From a Giddy Kipper at Ulverston'.
A giddy kipper is a foolish or lovesick person, hence the picture of the loving couple in the middle.

First published in the United Kingdom, 2003,
by Stenlake Publishing
01290 551122
www.stenlake.co.uk

ISBN 9781840332568

FURTHER READING

The books listed below were used by the author during her research. None of them are available from Stenlake Publishing. Those interested in finding out more are advised to contact their local bookshop or reference library.

D. Ashburner, *A Story of the Growth of Ulverston*, Fletcher & Robinson, 1995
L. R. Ayre, ed., *North Lonsdale Magazine and Furness Miscellany*, Vols. 1–4, W. Holmes, 1894–1901
The Barrow and District Year Book, 1913, *Barrow News & Mail*
J. Marsh & J. Garbutt, *Ulverston – A Nostalgic View of a Market Town*, Faust Publications, 1989
H. W. Mackereth & W. Holmes, *Furness Year Book*, 1895–1909
Oxley Development Co. Ltd., *Robert Frederick Oxley, A Scientific Businessman*, 1990

ACKNOWLEDGEMENTS

I would like to thank my late father for leaving me his local history books, which provided great help with the captions, and also my uncles Eric and Geoff Randall who gave me a few local tales. The majority of the pictures came from my great aunt Margaret Hornsby's collection, salvaged from 20 Alexander Road in the 1960s by my mother Eileen Randall and myself, who rescued what treasured things we could transport by bus before they were sold out of the family. Although a number of the pictures are family photographs, I have included them as they provide an insight into different aspects of life in Ulverston in an era that has now long since passed.

The publishers and author would like to thank John Garbutt for reading over the manuscript, and Francis Shuttleworth for providing the pictures and captions on pages 16 and 17.

INTRODUCTION

Ulverston is guarded by Hoad Monument, which dominates any view of the town. On a Thursday it is seen to be a thriving small market town with a character all of its own, nestling below the mighty Cumbrian mountains to the north.

No account of the village of Ulverston is found before the Norman Conquest, at which point the Domesday Book was commissioned by William the Conqueror. In 1537, at the same time as the dissolution of Furness Abbey near Dalton in Furness, Ulverston was surrendered to Henry VIII, and at the time was described as having eleven residents occupying a single tenement with mills and gardens. The village initially grew as a market town, being situated at a location where several routes met. A number of farms were also centred there, but industry increased in the 1700s with weaving, tanning and iron-making being carried on within Ulverston's boundaries.

With the opening of the Ulverston Canal in 1796, shipbuilding expanded along with rope-making, bone- and paper-milling and tanning, leading to a rise in population of 10% over a ten year period. Between 1851 and 1891 Ulverston's population underwent another significant increase: from 6,742 to approximately 10,000. This was mainly made possible due to expansion of the railway network. John Brogden leased several of the haematite iron ore mines in the area but had difficulty in transporting their output. One of his four sons, Alexander, was an engineer who had been involved in railway projects in other parts of the country. He joined forces with his father to build a line through Ulverston (there was already an isolated single-track line running from Ulverston to Roa Island where the iron was collected by boat). Brogden and his son succeeded in linking Ulverston with the national railway network at Carnforth, although the exercise proved to be a considerable financial burden on the family who had to involve another engineer, James Brunlees, to deal with the difficult terrain over which the Leven viaduct passed. The line was finally opened in 1857 and was doubled in 1860. However, in 1862 the Furness Railway Company came to the financial aid of the Brogdens, effectively taking over operation of the line from that time. The current Ulverston station, designed by Paley & Austin, opened in 1874.

The canal and the railway brought increased industrialisation to Ulverston, with the ironworks at south Ulverston established in 1874. In addition to this there were six shipyards and several smaller industrial concerns such as breweries, tanneries, brickworks, sail works and ropeworks. In the area around the canal there was a wire-works, a chemical works and several quarries. Many of these industries dwindled away in the 1920s and 30s.

Randall & Porter used Low Mill, an old cotton mill, as a tanyard between 1890 and the 1960s and were a major employer in the town during some difficult periods in its history. Glaxo came to Ulverston in 1948 to establish a large factory to make penicillin and soon after streptomycin, occupying the site of Ulverston's old ironworks. With a worldwide reputation in pharmaceuticals already established, the company has proved a key employer in the town. In the 1980s the factory was expanded to make ceftazidime, which is used to treat a wide range of bacterial infections. Many products have been manufactured at the factory during its existence and in 1998 five so-called principal products were being made on the Ulverston site.

Most of Ulverston's town centre has retained its old-world charm, with many streets having changed little over the last two centuries. Today it is attracting tourists by promoting itself as a festival town with regular events such as the banner, folk, lantern and Dickensian festivals. Ulverston is the birthplace of Stan Laurel of Laurel and Hardy fame, and there is a small private museum dedicated to this fact.

The town's heritage is being preserved by a voluntary society of enthusiasts, who are presently looking for a home in which to display their artefacts. A large glass factory outlet also welcomes tourists, while there are also several high-class art and craft shops and exhibition centres. The Welfare State International premises in the Ellers has received a design award for its notable renovation of an old building.

Service industries now play a major part in the area's economy, and many people are employed in retail, tourism and care-work. Apart from the pretty constant roar of the A590 – which divides the town in two – Ulverston is generally a quiet, sleepy town.

A fine turnout in Alexander Road, Ulverston, showing Maud, Jack and George Patrick from Durham visiting the Hornsbys at No. 20. Arthur Kellet from Tarnside is at the reins. The Patricks came to Ulverston every year for the North Lonsdale Rose Society Exhibition which was held annually in Todbusk Park in July. Established in 1894, it was regarded as one of the most fashionable fêtes of the late Victorian and Edwardian eras. The ornate railings in front of the houses were removed during the Second World War. Few were replaced afterwards.

Arthur Kellet is seen here driving Mrs Margaret Hornsby back to Alexander Road. Arthur lived alone in Tarnside and worked part-time as a postman as well as being a driver for the Hornsby family. He looked after Lucy, the family horse, which was stabled in a field in Stockbridge Lane. Arthur's wage for the driving and livery was the princely sum of five shillings a week.

The drawing room of 20 Alexander Road was on the first floor at the front of the house. Its full name was the withdrawing room, and it was here that the ladies retired after dinner while the men decamped to the smoking room on the ground floor. This photograph of Miss Margaret Hornsby shows her taking afternoon tea, complete with starched tablecloth, silver-plated teapot and Belleek teacups. The whatnot in the corner was painted gold and the cake stand was made of bamboo and stretched lace. Margaret is wearing a white cotton tea gown with Irish lace insertions, pin-tucks and starched frills, while a lavish shawl is draped over the back of the chair. Robert Hornsby, who owned the house, moved to Ulverston from Durham in 1843 to become the local postmaster. Margaret was his daughter and took over the post when he retired. She herself retired in 1917. Robert and his wife had six children: Reveley (who drowned at sea when he was taking his Masters Certificate); Jack and Alfred (both of whom emigrated to America); Percy (who went to the Yukon); Margaret; and Arabella.

This handsome man about town was my great uncle, Percy Hornsby, who went out to Dawson City in 1897 at the time of the gold rush known as the Klondike stampede. He made his life there and fought with the Canadian army during the First World War. Percy used to come back to Ulverston periodically to see his relatives in Alexander Road. This portrait was taken by J. Hargreaves, a prolific photographer who had studios in Ulverston, Dalton, Barrow and Millom.

This photograph shows the timber cabin in Dawson City where Percy lived. He never married and made his living prospecting for gold – on his visits home to Ulverston he often bought back large nuggets of gold and when he had spent up would return to the Yukon. He had a reputation for living hard and playing hard. Not all of those who went to Dawson City made their fortune, but Percy Hornsby managed to earn a living from prospecting until his death in 1931.

This second view of the drawing room at 20 Alexander Road shows it during Victorian times. The Hornsbys bought this house as it was large enough to accommodate a family of eight. They hired help for cleaning and laundry from the town, but did not have any live-in staff. Robert Hornsby's daughter Arabella married a Mr Hood and had two children, a boy and a girl called Reveley and Gladys. Arabella helped run two draper's shops in London but after her husband died she moved back to Ulverston to look after her ailing parents. Reveley died of peritonitis aged eight. Gladys went to school at Springfield Mansion, a small private school for young ladies (see page 41), before going on to study music and singing at the Paris Conservatoire. She married a Scotsman, Peter Morrow from Perth, who had come to the area to work in the shipyard in Barrow-in-Furness. He died of tuberculosis when his children Dennis and Eileen were very young. Gladys then worked as a nurse and her mother, Arabella, brought up the two children in the family home in Alexander Road. During the 1930s lodgers were taken in to help with the household costs at a time when there were no male family members to bring in a wage.

Having lost their father at a young age, Dennis and Eileen Morrow went to an orphanage boarding school called Reedham; this photograph was taken in Ulverston during a visit home. Reedham was a charitable institution that had previously been called the Asylum of Fatherless Children. Its first home was a large house on the banks of the River Thames at Richmond, but it moved several times, always to locations in or around London. The children only had holidays in summer and at Christmas and Eileen remembers feeling very homesick for Ulverston. Her mother, Gladys, used to take nursing jobs in London so she could visit. This was frowned upon so the visits had to be clandestine and took place in the school's wooded grounds. The car in the photograph belonged to Mr Broomby, owner of a builders' yard at the end of the road in the 1920s, 30s and 40s. Broomby's is still one of the largest builders merchants in the area and is now located on North Lonsdale Road.

Dennis Morrow photographed in a three-wheeled Bond mini car in the 1950s before he emigrated to Canada (there was widespread emigration after the Second World War). Dennis served in the merchant navy in the Atlantic during the Second World War. The lady next to him in the car was his wife-to-be, Betty. Dennis Morrow became a draughtsman after serving his time at Vickers Shipbuilders in Barrow-in-Furness. The apprenticeships were so good then that it was said that after serving your time at Vickers you could get a job anywhere in the world. Dennis died in 2002 aged 85.

Margaret Hornsby (seen also in the picture on page 5) photographed at the back of Kirklands, the house which she rented from the Kennedy family of Stone Cross House after moving out of the family home in Alexander Road. Like her father before her, Margaret was postmistress in Ulverston for a number of years and people in the town still remember her as a feisty character. She was engaged to a local solicitor called Mr Hart Jackson for many years but they never married due to his sons' objections. Apparently she had a chaise longue in the back room of the post office, which was the talk of the neighbourhood at the time because she entertained her fiance there.

The lady standing in the porch of Lund Hall in this view was an Austrian countess who was asked to move away from her home after a scandal which involved Crown Prince Rudolf Habsburg, the son of Emperor Franz Joseph and Empress Elisabeth of Austria, shooting himself and his lover, Mary Vetsera, at the royal hunting lodge in Mayerling on 30 January 1889. Unfortunately the name of the disgraced countess has not been confirmed, but a Countess Marie Larisch was forced into exile after the Mayerling affair because she had introduced Mary and Rudolf and admitted serving as a go-between for the couple. However, there is no record of her moving to England, so she is unlikely to be the person in question. Although the details are vague, the lady in the picture had arrived at Lund Hall by 1900. She had various gentlemen friends, one of whom, Mr Atkinson (pictured here), she lived with. Around the time of the outbreak of the First World War she left Lund Hall, possibly to be interned due to her links with enemy countries. This card was sent to Margaret Hornsby, the postmistress, with whom – judging by the tone of the greeting – she was very friendly. My grandmother, Gladys Morrow, remembered visiting the house with her aunt. At the time rugs made from wild animal skins – complete with heads and paws – were fashionable and Gladys recalled tripping over the lion and tiger heads on the floor.

Kirklands, the house that Margaret Hornsby lived in after she moved out of Alexander Road, is seen here on the left before the A590 was built in front of Holy Trinity Church (right). In the early nineteenth century all of Ulverston's population of 4,000 would have been expected to attend church, although many were unable to do this due to the limited capacity of St Mary's Parish Church, which was the only C. of E. place of worship in the expanding town at the time. With the help of Colonel Gale-Braddyll of Conishead Priory, the Revd John Sunderland brought about the building of Holy Trinity Church in the south of the town. The first service was held there on 25 March 1832. The Kennedys, who owned much of the land and mineral rights in the area, commissioned windows for the church in memory of members of their family. The final one was commissioned in 1884 by the last Mrs Kennedy to live at Stone Cross House, and was in memory of her husband Myles. From 1873 the vicar of Holy Trinity was the Revd Canon Ayre. He and his wife were instrumental in fund-raising and setting up Sunday schools in Ulverston. Holy Trinity ceased to be a church in 1975 after which the building became a leisure club for a while. It has since been converted into apartments.

Taken by local photographer S. S. Crewdson, this photograph shows a newly-built Rock House on the corner of Alexander Road. The house is still standing and was in use as a hotel until recently. The gap between Rock House and the smaller dwellings to the right of it was later filled in with two more terraced houses. A garage now occupies the space in the foreground. Mr Crewdson's studio was in Union Street.

This postcard was sent from 5 Stanley Mount (shown in the background of the view) in 1907. In those days there were cottages in front of and to the side of Stanley Mount. When the property was bought by James Randall in 1913 he had some of the cottages demolished in order to make more room for a larger garden and car parking. Geoffrey Randall, his son, recounted how one day a large hole appeared in the garden where the builders had not filled in the cellar of one of the cottages. James lived in Stanley Mount until his death in 1945. It has now been split into two houses.

The Kennedy family owned most of the iron ore mines in the Furness area and lived in Stone Cross House. This picture shows the drawing room of Stone Cross before the Second World War. The family were very active socially and opened up their house and grounds for a variety of charitable functions. For instance on 24 and 25 June 1910 they held a country fair in aid of the fund for the treatment of consumptives from North Lonsdale in the Meathop Sanatorium. Eileen Morrow, my mother, remembers visiting Stone Cross with her aunt in the 1920s and Mrs Kennedy sweeping down the staircase in full-length widow's weeds.

This tranquil rural scene shows the view from Hoad Hill looking out over Next Ness Farm and Causeway End. What is now the busy A590 road is hidden by the high foreground. At the time these narrow country lanes were still used by horses and carts. Tridley Point and the Leven viaduct can be seen jutting into Morecambe Bay.

This early Crewdson photograph looks east from Hoad Hill and shows the ironworks, canal and railway bridge. Myles Kennedy of Stone Cross in Ulverston was a major shareholder in the ironworks. Hot slag from the furnaces was tipped on the site where the Glaxo sports club and fields are now located. According to my mother the glow from this was bright enough to read by at night time. In the 1930s she stayed in a little row of cottages by Ulverston ironworks with her school friend, Betty Guthrie, whose father was manager of the works. The cottages are no longer standing.

The Furness Railway line from Barrow to Ulverston was opened in stages from 1846, Ulverston station finally being opened on 7 June 1854. The present station (above), in Italianate style and with a tall clock tower was built in 1874. *Photograph by F. W. Shuttleworth.*

North Lonsdale signal box. The line from Ulverston to Carnforth was opened by the Ulverston & Lancaster Railway on 10 August 1857 for goods traffic and on 1 September that year for passenger traffic. The line was absorbed into the Furness Railway in 1862. *Photograph by F. W. Shuttleworth.*

By 1774 Ulverston had become established as a port and had 70 ships registered as belonging to it. Thomas Sunderland came to the town from Haverthwaite in 1780 and quickly took a leading role in its affairs. He formed a committee with a group of local businessmen to improve the town's facilities by building a canal, becoming the chairman of the enterprise and cutting the first sod in 1793. The surveyor was John Rennie, who had built the first Waterloo Bridge in London. The canal cost over £4,000 in total, and opened in 1796; it is famous for being the deepest, straightest and shortest canal in England. It led to an increase in the shipbuilding that was carried out at Saltcoates Sandside by William Ashburner and Ephraim Swainson. At the same time the rope and twine industry developed, and Ulverston had two rope-walks, one of which is still visible at Outcast. The canalside spawned a tannery, bone mill and paper mill. The canal's busiest year was 1846 when more than 940 ships passed through its gates.

Ulverston ironworks was established in 1874 and used the canal to transport raw materials and finished products via vessels such as the *City of Liverpool*. She was owned by the works and used Ainslie Pier for the loading and unloading of iron ore and pig iron. This activity helped to keep the canal busy at a time when railways were gradually eroding water-borne freight traffic, although in 1916 channel movements in Morecambe Bay meant that sea freight became even less viable and use of the canal by shipping ceased. The North Lonsdale Iron & Steel Co. Ltd. continued to operate throughout the Great Depression of the 1930s, but by 1938 only one furnace was being used and the works closed in the late 40s. Luckily for Ulverston, the site was quickly taken over by Glaxo pharmaceuticals. They gradually smoothed the slag banks to make playing fields and space for more factory buildings. Waste from the ironworks also helped to build flood defences from the sea.

Treatment of tuberculosis patients at High Carley Sanatorium in the 1930s involved plenty of fresh air, and so the hospital was designed with many verandas. Gladys Morrow, my grandmother, nursed there even though she had been left a widow by TB (or consumption as it was commonly known) in the 1920s with two small children to support. Her son Dennis had tuberculosis in his neck but survived. In the days before inoculations were developed the illness claimed many lives.

Stanley Street workhouse was built in 1836 and provided a welfare service of sorts for the area until 5 January 1948 when the National Health Service was born and it was turned into a hospital. It had accommodation for 350 'paupers'. These were people who could not find work or support themselves, such as orphans, the elderly and unmarried mothers. Eileen Randall remembers seeing the 'inmates' walking round town in pairs, crocodile fashion. The work involved cleaning and gardening etc. and the workhouse was a hated and feared place, with a dreadful stigma attached to it. This postcard showing the dining hall cheerfully decorated for Christmas in 1904 belies the workhouse's more institutional image.

Ulverston Cottage Hospital was built on garden ground in Newton Street donated by Myles Kennedy the elder. It opened in 1873 and catered mainly for casualty patients until 1906 when it started to take surgical cases and developed a maternity department. Prior to the foundation of the welfare state after the Second World War, hospitals were funded by voluntary contributions rather than the state, and fund-raising through public events such as the parade featured opposite was vital.

The annual parade in aid of the local cottage hospital dates from 1899 and traditionally takes place on the first Saturday in July. It is still going strong today, with money raised now donated to local charities. This picture shows the 1906 parade gathering in the Gill before setting off around the town. The money raised during that year's parade made a significant contribution to the hospital's running costs, as well as providing funds for the development of new operating theatres and other capital projects. Case's Ales, whose float is in the foreground, had a large brewery in Barrow-in-Furness.

This photograph shows the aftermath of the fire at the County Hotel, a major event in 1911. Eric Randall lived in Brogden Street at the time and remembers his father wrapping him up in an eiderdown to watch the fire from their window during the night. J. Hargreaves took this photograph of the burnt-out hotel and sold it as a postcard. Between 1900 and 1939 many photographers and printers published their own postcards – at the time the post was fast and reliable and postcards were a very cheap form of communication. The Coronation Hall, affectionately known as 'The Coro', stands on the site once occupied by the hotel. Built to commemorate the coronation of King George V, it is one of Ulverston's principal buildings.

The Coronation Hall and adjoining post office were built on the site of the County Hotel in 1914 and are still in use now. The interior of the hall provides a glimpse of Britain's extensive influence at the time, with friezes above the stage showing Britannia and images of the colonies. Prior to this date Ulverston's post office was located in the office used by Hart Jackson's solicitors in New Market Street. A roundabout planted with flowers is now situated in the area in the foreground where the cars are parked.

Celebrations in honour of Queen Victoria's Diamond Jubilee were held on 22 June 1897 when a marvellous pageant thronged the streets of Ulverston. The town was decorated with banners, flags and streamers and at 11 a.m. the volunteers, fire brigade, friendly societies and local schoolchildren assembled in the Gill and sang the national anthem, accompanied by the volunteer band. At 12 o'clock the volunteers fired a *feu de joie* (rifle salute) in the County Square. On returning, the schoolchildren received a jubilee mug, a new sixpence and a bag of cakes. At 10 p.m. a huge bonfire was lit on Outrake hill. It was 37 feet high and 27 feet in diameter, and burned throughout the night. Other bonfires could be seen in the vicinity at Yarlside, Hawcoat and Bardsea. This photograph graphically illustrates the size of the Ulverston bonfire.

In 1906 G. B. Haddock, a Liverpool shipowner and director of Lindal Moor iron ore mines, stood as the Unionist candidate for North Lonsdale, advocating a policy of protectionism. He was unexpectedly elected to Parliament, unseating Richard Cavendish of Holker Hall, the Liberal candidate who stood for free trade. The polling day was reported to have passed off with no disruptions, although the noise of motor cars and carriages was noted as being much in evidence.

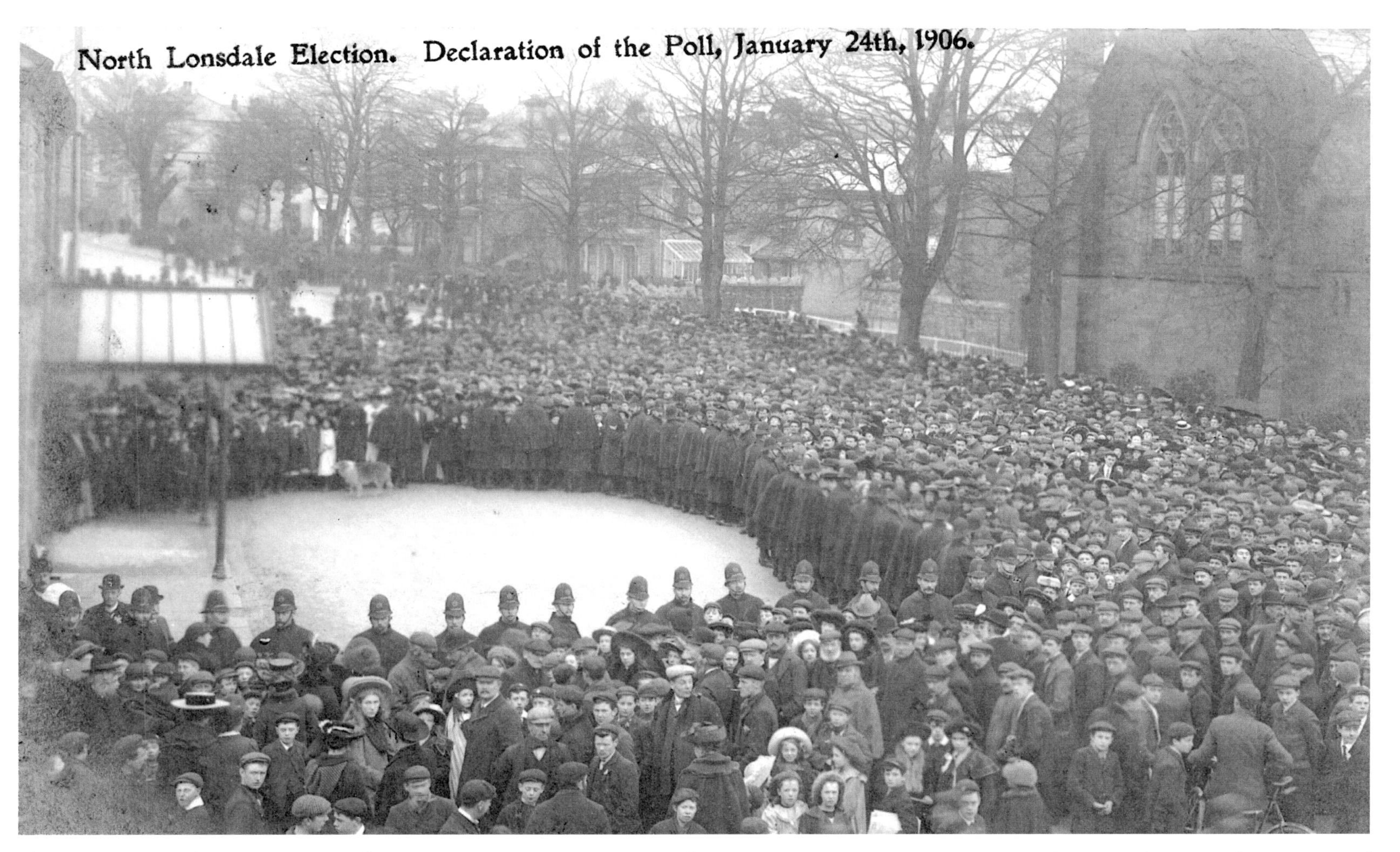

The declaration of the poll took place the next day, on 24 January, outside the Drill Hall in Victoria Road. It was a close-run election with a majority of only 179. Interest in the event was high, with a large police presence seen here holding back the crowd. G. B. Haddock himself sent this postcard on 8 February 1906. It is addressed to a Miss Dixon of Stonelands Farm, Field Broughton, Grange-over-Sands. No candidates represented any other political parties as there was felt to be little support for them in the area. Mr Haddock's election expenses were £1,230 14s 3d – a considerable sum in those days.

Atkinson's printing and stationery business was founded in 1836 by David Atkinson, a farmer's son from Gawthwaite. The printing side of the business was conducted from a double fronted warehouse in Upper Brook Street which is now a shop. The last Atkinson, George, never married, so after his retirement the business was sold, and in 1949 the King Street shop (above) became a bookshop owned by two keen local historians, Geoffrey and Nan Randall. During the early twentieth century most printers and stationers sold photographic postcards that they produced themselves, and on taking over the premises the Randalls gave the old stock of Atkinson postcards to Ulverston Heritage Centre.

This Edwardian view of King Street shows the shops on the other side of the street from Atkinson's, with Noblett's Everton Toffee Shop, which became Katy Crawford's in the 1920s, in the left foreground. Everton Toffee was made by A. Beer & Co. Ltd. in Ulverston. 'Beer's toffees are guaranteed genuine toffees, are cut in dainty pieces, and each piece daintily wrapped in wax paper, on which the name of Beer's is printed as a guarantee of their quality.' The building protruding slightly on the right was the Hare and Hounds pub, which later became a potter's shop with a tiled facade and eventually finished up as the Inglenook Cafe. The premises were later demolished.

This postcard was sent in 1909 and shows the Queen's Hotel on the left with what is probably John Jackson's cart (see opposite) being loaded up outside. The King's Arms is facing the camera. At the time the King's was nicknamed 'the Klondike', as this was shortly after the era of the gold rush in the Yukon and the landlord had a large and greatly admired gold fob watch.

The well-known carrier John Jackson lived in Water Yeat. On a Thursday the pubs were open all day for market day. John liked his drink and having had a skinful would be put in the back of his cart at which point his horses – who knew the route by heart – would take him back home. When he bought a Model T Ford, he was asked what he thought of it. 'Nae good,' was his reply, 'It won't ga yam!' (It won't go home). His stand in Ulverston was outside the Queen's Hotel in King Street and on Tuesdays, Thursdays and Saturdays he carried all manner of goods between Ulverston, Pennybridge, Greenodd, Lowick, Blawith, Sparkbridge, Torver and Coniston.

The view along King Street from Market Square in the 1920s. The firm of Ruddick's (formerly Hird's) closed in 1938 at which point my grandmother bought up their entire stock of tinned foods, which came in very useful during the war years. This building became the premises of Robert Oxley, who single-handedly founded Oxley Developments Ltd. in Ulverston after his first workshop and office in London was bombed in the blitz. His work was considered so important that he was instructed to go to a safe area away from German bombs. Oxley designed and manufactured small components for the communications industry, and the Ministry of Aircraft Production instructed him to supply them with essential parts needed for the war effort. After the war he moved his enterprise to Priory Park, a large Victorian manor house where he went on to develop new designs, methods and processes not only for the military but in a wide range of devices that he marketed himself. In 1978 he set up another company, Telecommunications Research and Development on the Isle of Man, for the production of light-emitting diodes. R. F. Oxley established ancillary companies in Zurich, South Africa, and America.

A postcard of a busy Market Square (looking into Market Street) sent in 1909 and showing H. W. Mackereth's premises. Between 1895 and 1909 the firm issued the popular annual *Furness Year Book*.

Gillam's shop (right) was a so-called cash grocers situated in Market Street. Before the Second World War most grocers would give customers 'tick' or goods on account, although the description 'cash grocer' indicated that Gillam's didn't offer credit. In those shops that did supply items on tick, accounts were usually payable quarterly and deliveries were made direct to customers' homes by bike or van. During the 1920s Gillam's had sacks of dried fruit outside the shop and children would sometimes dip into these on their way home from school.

Following the end of the First World War in 1918, this tank arrived in Ulverston and was placed in the square at the bottom of Market Street, after which it came to be known as Tank Square. The tank was scrapped during the Second World War.

County Square seen before the A590 was built through this part of the town. Birkett's County Stores was a large department store selling mostly clothes. The premises are now occupied by an estate agents and solicitor's office.

Conishead Priory is a Gothic-style mansion situated on the route to Bardsea. Work on it began in 1821 and it took fifteen years and £140,000 to complete, putting such financial strain on its owner, Colonel Wilson Gale-Braddyll, that the house and lands had to be sold to pay his debts. It was later used as a hydropathic hotel, serving as such until 1933 at which point the Durham Miners' Association opened it as a convalescent home. In the 1960s and 70s it was left empty and its structure deteriorated badly. A group of Tibetan monks took over the task of restoring the house and gardens, now known as the Manjushri Mahayana Buddhist Centre. The order have built a temple in the grounds where devotees gather every year from all over the world. A priory was originally established on this site during the reign of Henry II (1154–89), at which time it was home to the Black Friars, who were Augustinian monks. They took care of lepers and other unfortunates at the priory until the dissolution of the monasteries by Henry VIII in 1537. There was a Gothic-style hall on the site until 1820 which was occupied by succeeding generations of landed gentry – their family names were Monteagle, Paget, Machell, Sandys, Dodding and Braddyll.

Sir John Barrow was born in 1765, the son of a journeyman tanner. His birthplace, this small thatched cottage at Dragley Beck, has survived and is now owned by the local council which rents it out. Barrow was educated at the Town Bank Grammar School where he proved to be a genius at mathematics and astronomy. He became a seafaring explorer after whom Point Barrow in Alaska (which he discovered), Barrow Sound and Barrow Bay at the north-western tip of North America (in Ontario, Canada) are named. During his 40 year career at the Admiralty (to which he became Secretary), he published several articles in scientific journals, and also wrote an account of the mutiny on the *Bounty*. Barrow was made a baronet in 1835 for services to his country. After his death in 1848 two local worthies, Alexander Brogden and Robert Hannay, bought his cottage in Ulverston and donated it to his son. He in turn gave it to the town council.

This photograph shows members of one of the Higher Grade's rugby teams before the school lost a number of its pupils to the upper school in 1930. Some of the individuals can be identified. *Back row:* fourth from left, James (Jim) Randall; fourth from right, Joe Delamere (later taught at Ulverston Grammar School); right-hand end, Jimmy Langtree. *Front row:* second from left, Bernard White; centre, Dr Cousins (headmaster); third from right, Jimmy Grundy.

Ulverston Grammar School hockey team 1935/36, with Eileen Morrow (my mother) on the left. She played right wing for the school, Ulverston Hockey Club and the county of Westmorland. Marion Phillips played left wing and is seated on the right of the group. She married Billy Wolfenden who also played hockey. Although the Furness region north of the sands was technically part of Lancashire, in those days Westmorland separated it geographically so it joined with Westmorland for county hockey. Eileen and her husband James Randall restarted the Ulverston Hockey Club after the Second World War when many teams amalgamated due to lack of players. The English headed sticks illustrated in the picture are very different to those used today with their tiny heads.

This wedding took place at Ulverston Parish Church during the Second World War. The groom was Captain James Lister Randall of the Durham Light Infantry, who fought in Sicily and North Africa with the 8th Army. He was taken from his sick bed to lead a troop into France on D-Day and was taken ill again soon afterwards, eventually losing one of his kidneys as a result of drinking bad water in the desert campaign. His bride was Eileen Morrow and her dress was made from curtain material with an over bodice of Brussels lace taken from her mother's wedding dress. The weather was so cold on the day of the wedding, 7 March 1942, that Eileen's veil froze to the ground. Jim arrived the night before and the couple only had a few days in a Keswick hotel before he had to return to active duty. Dennis Morrow (second from the right), Eileen's brother, gave her away and Eric Randall, the groom's elder brother, was the best man. The bridesmaids were Agnes Perry, left, Eileen's workmate from the County Court in Barrow, and Helen Ronaldson, her friend from school (Reedham in Surrey), who was in the ATS (Auxiliary Territorial Service) in London and manned an anti-aircraft gun.

The autumn one-day motorcycle trial took place under the auspices of the Auto-cycle Union in the Lake District on 2 November 1912. James Randall, who owned the Low Mill tanyard in Ulverston, had many interests and helped organise this event. He is seen here second from the right with a 2.5 horsepower Sunbeam motorcycle. The other cycles are, from left to right, a Zenith, a Rudge, a Premier and a Swift. The location is the Monk Coniston to Tarn Hows road and the men had gathered to prepare for the forthcoming motorcycle trial.

In the *Westmorland Gazette*, the trial was described as 'the most severe test in the history of motor cycling, the route selected being through the roughest part of the Lake District and covering a distance of over 100 miles. Undoubtedly the stiffest test was the climb out of the Langdale valley. Of 55 riders only five succeeded in getting up it. The surface was exceedingly loose and treacherous. Never before had so many of the cleverest and most experienced riders been brought to a standstill. It can well be imagined that the bottom part of the hill was strewn with riders and machines that could make no headway. Engines were racing, back wheels spinning and clouds of blue smoke issuing from the hard-pressed engines.' The five riders to make it out of the valley were S. Crawley (Triumph); J. Bushby (Alldays), J. R. Alexander (Indian), and C. T. Newsome and D. H. Noble on Rovers.

Another of James Randall's passions was motor cars. Here he is seen driving his Wolseley on a family outing in the lakes. This must have been a posed photograph as James was always chauffeur-driven. His daughter Edith Randall is at his side.